$\blacklozenge \blacklozenge \blacklozenge$ FOR $\blacklozenge \blacklozenge \blacklozenge$

❖ THE ❖
FRIENDSHIP
QUILT

Piecin' a Quilt is Like
Livin' a Life

◆ ◆ ◆ ◆ ◆ ◆ ◆

Compiled by
Esther L. Beilenson

Illustrated and Designed by
Mullen & Katz

PETER PAUPER PRESS, INC.
WHITE PLAINS, NEW YORK

For Sarah and Hannah

Copyright © 1997
Peter Pauper Press, Inc.
202 Mamaroneck Avenue
White Plains, NY 10601
All rights reserved
ISBN 0-88088-200-X
Printed in Singapore
7 6 5 4 3 2 1

CONTENTS

INTRODUCTION

A patchwork quilt is like life. It is made up of many small pieces that together have a history, and add up to all the days of your life.

The quilt may be made of odd bits of wedding dresses from mothers and grandmothers, from bits of silk ties, remnants of cloth left over from patterns, pieces of old jeans—or even, especially today, from store-bought fabric.

It may be the creation of a solitary artist, and her choice of fabric, intricacy and beauty of design, and expert stitching may make her quilt a true artistic treasure.

A quilt may, however, evidence the stitches of many hands, from a quilting society or a group of neighboring women. Early on, in frontier towns or farming communi-

ties, quilts were often stitched at quilting bees that were major social events in the lives of hardworking people. In the fabrics of the quilt and in the stitching itself (showing the differing personalities and talents of many hands) lie stories of the women who fashioned the quilts. Weddings and children, joys and sorrows, all speak out to us from these quilts.

Quilts are warm coverlets, and make beautiful wall coverings. They express the creativity and imagination of the makers. But, of greatest significance, they embody the forging of lifelong friendships among women.

E. L. B.

AMONG FRIENDS

If you put two quilters in the same room, no matter if they are parents, golfers, church members, or computer operators, they talk about quilts. Hooray for quilting. Hooray for friendships. Hooray for a creative, warm, wonderful way to celebrate them.

Helen Kelley

◆ ◆ ◆ ◆ ◆ ◆ ◆

We feel secure almost involuntarily within the group. Our individual talents are realized, and bonds of friendship are developed. We give and receive freely. In groups, designs become quilts, people become friends.

Mary Golden

◆ ◆ ◆ ◆ ◆ ◆ ◆

The passion I possess for my quilting comes from wanting to share my quilts with someone else. I wish I had the time to execute all of the ideas in my head.

Karen Schoepflin Hagen

All the quilters I've met are wonderful, easygoing, and helpful.

Arthur A. Bluj

◆ ◆ ◆ ◆ ◆ ◆ ◆

[There is the sociable side to quilting.] I meet many interesting people with common goals and feel that I am also able to touch people's lives at times with my quilting.

Patricia Cooper

◆ ◆ ◆ ◆ ◆ ◆ ◆

For me, an important aspect of quilting lies in the opportunities for shared work, learning, and achievement. The attraction of quilting extends to all ages, all walks of life. It is an important activity, because it helps me to form friendships with younger people and to break out of the tendency to live in limited contact with only older people.

Lucy Hilty

◆ ◆ ◆ ◆ ◆ ◆ ◆

Aunt Argie Stem collected scraps for her Double Wedding Ring quilt from students at the Rover one-room school. Everyone had a part in her quilt.

Barbara Crockett Troxler

Since quiltmaking is often a solitary effort, the moments spent with friends talking, enjoying, admiring, and dreaming quilts are most precious.

Vivian Ritter

The first quilt I ever made I took with me everywhere, and I found that working on this quilt at school board meetings allowed old family, old rancher coastal people who saw me as kind of a radical, almost troublemaker, perhaps, [to see me in a different light]. The quilt became a bridge where they would come up to me and say "my grandmother made that quilt. She made that same pattern, it was different colors." Suddenly there's this bond between people who may not have other things in common.

Susanna Calderon

◆ ◆ ◆ ◆ ◆ ◆ ◆

[The Wetlands Institute Quilters] have so enjoyed the weekly get-togethers that they give up a week to the Christmas holiday season only with reluctance.

Marion Glaspey

I have always sought out the community of quilt-makers, and my work has been nourished by the support and interest of friends.

Vikki Chenette

Some quilters have loved our meetings so much that they actually learned to drive so they would not have to miss one or depend on someone else to take them. Seeing so many women taking up this marvelous art form is really a lasting reward.

Anita Murphy

I can remember my mother and her friends, black and white, they all quilted together, and they would have meals together, and they would sit down and quilt this quilt together. We would go to each one's house, you come to my house today, round and round until we would make a circle. Sometimes we'd have three and four quilts. When you're piecing quilts you get to know each other, and you're more concerned about each other because you have a feeling for that person.

Nora Lee Condra

I have found that quilt lovers are special people. . . .
I am happy to be "at home" with my friends and quilts.
Joyce Gross

◆ ◆ ◆ ◆ ◆ ◆ ◆

Quilting is an artistic outlet for so many people,
and the wonderful thing is that there's room for everybody.
Brenda Duncan Shornick

◆ ◆ ◆ ◆ ◆ ◆ ◆

Are we good? You bet we are. That's what makes
the quilt. But some of our best quilters are getting rather
elderly and I guess we're down to about ten or twelve
really good quilters.
Jo Marner

◆ ◆ ◆ ◆ ◆ ◆ ◆

We all [at the Hansen Bee] share a sense of awe
concerning our quilting heritage—the social aspects, the
commitment given by women coping in a time when life
made a different set of demands, the innate sense of design
of quiltmakers long ago that still managed to affect us so
deeply, their workmanship, and the ability to foresee past
their own lives to a time when something they made
would live on—these things provide our inspiration.
Denise Sansing

Quilting has led me to new friends, to interesting places, and to personal satisfaction. It has brought me drawers overflowing with fabric, shelves drooping with books and magazines, corners filled with projects underway, and a mind busy with plans for the next project. It has filled my life in a very happy way. I am always busy and never bored.

Ann A. Shibut

◆ ◆ ◆ ◆ ◆ ◆ ◆

While my mother quilted, I would play under the quilt when it was hung in a frame. And when I wasn't playing under the quilt, my mother showed me how to push the needle in and out of the material.

Darlene Watson

◆ ◆ ◆ ◆ ◆ ◆ ◆

Quilting and quilt-related activities provide a certain continuity in my life. It is the one thing I do for myself. I sometimes tell people that I am a member of a worldwide underground network of women who hoard scraps of fabric!

Gloria Brown

Sometimes the thread gets knotted and must be carefully untangled. Even as our lives change and friends drift apart, the quilt remains in our possession. If we have followed the designer's plan, the quilt will be an enduring masterpiece which captures the essence of friendship.

Margie Boesch

♦ ♦ ♦ ♦ ♦ ♦ ♦

We are diverse in many ways, but quilting is the interest that has made us friends.

Janet Manahan

LINKS IN A CHAIN

This quilt's a piece of livin' history. It speaks to me in voices long passed away.

An Upsher County, WV, quilter

♦ ♦ ♦ ♦ ♦ ♦

Like my paintings, quilting is a record of my family, my life, and my interests.

Anita Holman Knox

♦ ♦ ♦ ♦ ♦ ♦

The new quilt was made by my daughter. The old one was pieced by my greatgrandmother and given to my mother. And she gave it to me. When I was a child, mother would take the quilt and spread it out. And she'd tell us stories of the pieces. This was Aunt So-and-so's dress. And that was So-and-so's wedding dress. . . . I don't rightly know how old it is. Well over a hundred years. My mother's ninety-two. And her grandmother pieced the quilt and was dead before she was ever born.

Mrs. Blanche Griffith

My grandmother was 98 when she passed. Before she passed away she would always tell me about her quilts. She would tell me that she wanted me to give each one of my children a quilt, and I had seven children . . . So she said give each one a quilt and then give my two brothers a quilt. She had enough to do that and then some over, and then she said the rest of them I was to keep for myself. Sometimes I get to thinking about her and I just look at the quilts and it makes me feel that she's close by. Because this is something she liked to do and it's something she did by hand.

Nora Lee Condra

◆ ◆ ◆ ◆ ◆ ◆ ◆

SUNNING QUILTS

Out from their scented chests I draw
And hand my bright quilts in the sun,
Fashioned by deft and patient hands
Whose work-days now are done.

This Irish Chain in vivid rose
Was Great-Aunt Phoebe's hope and pride—
Dear little girl, who died too young
To be a happy bride.

These colors, with fair stitches joined
To form a bold True-Lovers' Knot,
Were lame Aunt Miriam's—in their glow
Her dull days she forgot.

My strong grandmother, unto whom
Life brought most bitter grief and smart,
Piecing this flower basket learned
To mend a broken heart.

Dead kinsfolk, who have left to me
These quilts you made in vanished springs,
Would that I had your fortitude
Your joy in simple things!

   Effie Smith Ely

♦ ♦ ♦ ♦ ♦ ♦ ♦

In East Tennessee, quilting has been a way of life for generations, and in days gone by, most designs used small bits of fabric left over from sewing necessities. I have been collecting quilt patterns and sewing quilts for 50 years—since I was 8 years old—and have about 1000 old patterns.

Carrie Lou Huffaker

Day after day the pattern grew;
Each block was deftly set in place,
And rows of tiny stitches tell
A tale that time cannot efface.
From *The Patchwork Coverlet*

After our 2-1/2 year old daughter died in 1978, I walked up and down the aisles of a local craft store, wanting to make something in our daughter's memory. I decided that the time I would have given Erica I would give to making a quilt. The result was a cross stitch quilt, and Erica continues to lead me to quilting.

Sara Newberg King

Here is a scrap of her mother's blue calico. How lovingly her fingers shaped this diamond, and how she was thinking, as she stitched it in, of her she was soon to leave, to cast her lot with one who was more to her than father, mother, sister, or brother! In this square is a bit of bright pink cambric. 'Tis a piece of her baby brother's dress. He only lived till he had learned to lisp the names of sister and mother, and then God took him to dwell with Him. So she went on, day after day, adding square and diamond. We will not describe them all, though there are tender recollections connected with each one. Finally it was pronounced large enough. Then it was lined, marked out in that wonderful shell pattern, and made ready for the friends to quilt. . . .

From *Household*, October, 1881

♦ ♦ ♦ ♦ ♦ ♦ ♦

Grannie sits in her oaken chair
The firelight flits o'er her silvery hair,
The silent children around her sit,
As she pieces her patchwork coverlet;
She tells them her story of London Town,
And shows them the scraps of her bridal gown;
Each fragment there is a printed page,
With mem'ries written 'twixt youth and age.
From the old song, *Patchwork*

[My] quilt design has evolved through the years and many generations of the McGukin family. I am calling it Grandma's Favorite because I believe it would be approved by not only Grandma but also the old quilters who traditionally sat around working out their own special patterns.

Annie McGukin

◆ ◆ ◆ ◆ ◆ ◆

This design was pieced by my great-grandmother and handed down to my grandmother, then my mother, and finally to me. . . .

Julia Mae Trammell

◆ ◆ ◆ ◆ ◆ ◆

When the author of this book (*Dolls of Three Centuries*) and her sister, Frank, two years younger, were small girls, it was a joy to them to nestle down in their mother's bed before going to their own bed at night and listen to stories suggested to her by the old prints in the pieced quilt on her bed. Whose dress had that print been? When was it bought? Where? Who made it? How was it made, and where was it first worn?

Eleanor St. George

GRANDMA'S QUILT

With gentle and loving fingers
She caressed the well worn fold;
'Round each piece a mem'ry lingers
Like a sweet story often told.
Sylvia Summers Pierce

I guess you could say that I'm a fifth generation quilter. I didn't actually start quilting myself until about 12 years ago, but I always thought everybody's grandmother made quilts!

Carolee Knutson

◆　◆　◆　◆　◆　◆　◆

I was so young when my grandmother died that I did not feel a closeness to her. But . . . I have made a minute study of each square in the quilt and now feel a personal, loving relationship with her. Now I know where I inherited my love of animals, wildlife, and all aspects of nature.

Zenaide Florence McDaniels

GRANDMOTHER'S QUILT

"Some day,
We will have a square for you."
She would say; and to me, standing by her knee
In that old-fashioned sitting room
With its forgotten horsehair,
Flowered carpeting,
And firelit hearth
Of childhood memory,
She would explain
That homemade tapestry:

"That pretty printed one
Was once your mother's dress;
The pink, Aunt Julia's,
And the blue, a shirt of Uncle Will's;
While all the corners were begun
With Kansas scraps Aunt Hannah sent
From where the Indians live,
Beneath the prairie sun;
And that old piece of fancy cloth
Was Uncle Albert's vest,
And all those fill-ins at the seams
Were ties of Grandpa's,
Long, long years ago—"
　　Sarah Wilson Middleton

That quilt's a part of the family. It's come down from eldest daughter to eldest daughter since—oh, I couldn't rightly say when. Long before the War between the States.

Lewis County quilter

◆ ◆ ◆ ◆ ◆ ◆ ◆

The children and grandchildren soon spend the money grandpa leaves, but they hold on to the quilts grandma makes and hands down to them.

Claud Callan

Quilts . . . were highly prized. One is mentioned in a will recorded at the Jonesborough courthouse by Jacob Miller, Sr., a son of early settlers. Jacob married Elizabeth Range in 1798, and she made the Rose quilt sometime before her death in 1843. The will, which was signed and dated in 1857, reads in part:

> To my grand daughter who now lives with me,
> Mary Devault, I give and bequeath . . . my quilted
> quilt of the pattern known and called
> "Rose of Sharon." . . .

Elizabeth Range Miller

◆ ◆ ◆ ◆ ◆ ◆ ◆

Among the happy stories stitched into a quilt was one made of white satin. The girl who pieced it said it was made from pieces of her grandmother's wedding-gown, her mother's wedding-gown, and her own bridal dress! It was odd to see the various shades which the satin had taken on in the flight of years. Some of it was so yellow that it was corn-color. And we imagined that we could pick out the quality which made the oldest and the newest frock, just from the texture of the satin which changes with the fashions.

Elizabeth Rhodes

◆ ◆ ◆ ◆ ◆ ◆ ◆

Thanks to my mother's tender care
For she materials did prepare
and taught my hands to sew.
Eliza Ann Bruen,
from an Ohio sampler

We have 19 grand nieces and nephews. In 1961 we got the plan, the idea of making a quilt for each one of these 19 and we planned to do it in 10 years. Then we took a whole week for cutting pieces. We cut three quilts in that solid week, with no time out except for sleeping and eating. We give the quilts to the recipients when they marry, but if they get to the age of forty and haven't married we present it to them then.

Hortense and Christine Miller

Quilts are a continuing chain of history; I hope my quilts are treasured by future generations.

Jane Eakin

A Stitch Out of Time

The feminine love of color, the longing for decoration, as well as pride in skill of needlecraft, found riotous expression in quilt-making. Women reveled in intricate and difficult patchwork; they eagerly exchanged patterns with one another; they talked over the designs and admired pretty bits of calico and pondered what combinations to make, with far more zest than women ever discuss art or examine high art specimens together today.

Alice Morse Earl

◆ ◆ ◆ ◆ ◆ ◆ ◆

This afternoon 21 young ladies paid us a visit and assisted us in quilting . . . One quilt was completed in two days, Ruth and a friend sewing during the day, six neighbors helping in the evening. At the same time one of these quiltings was taking place, the men of the family held a husking bee.

Ruth Henshaw Bascomb, *early 1800s*

We have had deep snow. No teams passed for over three weeks, but as soon as the drifts could be broken through Mary Scott sent her boy Frank around to say she was going to have a quilting. Everybody turned out. . . . One of Mary's quilts she called "The Star and Crescent." I had never seen it before. She got the pattern from a Mrs. Lefferts, one of the new Pennsylvania Dutch families, and pieced it this winter. A lot of Dutch are taking up land here in the Reserve.

From a letter from an Ohio woman, 1841

Our young ladies of the present generation know little of the mysteries of "Irish chain," "rising star," "block work," or "Job's trouble," and would be as likely to mistake a set of quilting frames for clothes poles as for anything else. It was different in our younger days. Half a dozen handsome patchwork quilts were as indispensable then as a marriage portion.

T. S. Arthur,
Godey's Lady's Book, 1849

Accept this trifle that I send,
Not as a stranger, but a friend.
Charlotte N. Follett
Inscription from a quilt block, 1847

◆ ◆ ◆ ◆ ◆ ◆ ◆

Accept my friend this little pledge
Your love and friendship to engage
If ere we should be called to part
Let this be settled in your heart
That when this little peace you see
You ever will remember me
M. E. A.
Woodstock, 1847
Verse from a Friendship Quilt

◆ ◆ ◆ ◆ ◆ ◆ ◆

At your quilting, maids don't dally,
A maid who is quiltless at twenty-one,
Never shall greet her bridal sun!
From an old quilt

When I was a girl we did not quilt any of the "tops" we had made until we were ready to be married. A girl announced her engagement by having a "quilting bee" just like you have an announcement party today.

Mrs. E. E. Hardesty

◆ ◆ ◆ ◆ ◆ ◆ ◆

Should I be parted from thee
Look at this and think of me
May I twine a wreath for thee
Sacred to love and memory.
From an Album Quilt, 1852

◆ ◆ ◆ ◆ ◆ ◆ ◆

A failure to ask a neighbour to a raising, clearing, a chopping frolic, or his family to a quilting, was considered a high indignity; such an one, too, as required to be explained or atoned for at the next muster or county court. Each settler was not only willing but desirous to contribute his share to the general comfort and public improvement, and felt aggrieved and insulted if the opportunity to do so were withheld.

Dr. J. G. M. Ramsey, 1853

Our minister was married a year ago, and we have been piecing him a bed-quilt; and last week we quilted it. I always make a pint of going to quilting, for you can't be backbited to your face, that's a moral sertenty. . . .

Marietta Holley (known as Josiah Allen's Wife),
Godey's Lady's Book, July, 1868

◆ ◆ ◆ ◆ ◆ ◆ ◆

The frontier people were not without their social pleasures. Amusements were not frequent nor were they elaborate, but they were enjoyed all the more because they came so seldom. I recall spending a very enjoyable day at a quilting bee. While the fingers plied the needle, tongues were equally busy. . . .

Luvenia Conway Roberts,
Bride of a Texas Ranger, 1875

◆ ◆ ◆ ◆ ◆ ◆ ◆

The centre of attraction was in the parlor, where the old ladies, who used to go to "quilting-bees" when they were girls, sat around the big quilting-frame which belongs to the Society, with every now and then a young lady sandwiched in between them to thread their needles . . .

"Mrs. Kate Hunnibee's Diary,"
Column from the Hearth and Home Newspaper,
June 4, 1870

♦ ♦ ♦ ♦ ♦ ♦ ♦

Every young girl should piece one quilt at least to carry away with her to her husband's home, and if her lot happens to be cast among strangers, as is often the case, the quilt when she unfolds it will seem like the face of a familiar friend, and will bring up a whole host of memories, of mother, sister, friend, too sacred for us to intrude upon.

Good Housekeeping, April 14, 1888

One morning the postman brought me an invitation to a real Quilting Bee. I was so thrilled for I knew many of the quilters in the little town in Iowa. . . . Two quilts, the Compass and the Wedding Ring, were in frames on the long screened veranda. The day was ideal and everybody came. Yes, and they all came with baskets filled with the good things that farm women know how to prepare. Each one tried to outdo the other, and I guess they did. Such a jolly, good time we had!

Carlie Sexton, 1930

◆ ◆ ◆ ◆ ◆ ◆ ◆

PIECIN' A QUILT IS LIKE LIVIN' A LIFE

How much piecin' a quilt is like livin' a life! You can give the same kind of pieces to two persons, and one will make a "nine-patch" and one'll make a "wild goose chase," and there will be two quilts made out of the same kind of pieces, and jest as different as they can be. And that is jest the way with livin'. The Lord sends us the pieces, but we can cut them out and put 'em together pretty much to suit ourselves, and there's a heap more in the cuttin' out and the sewin' than there is in the caliker.

Eliza Calvert Hall

◆ ◆ ◆ ◆ ◆ ◆ ◆

Like songs we hear on the radio that conjure strong memories of a particular time and place, quilts help us recall that part of life that is sewn up into them.

Ami Simms

◆ ◆ ◆ ◆ ◆ ◆ ◆

In the Blue Ridge Mountains where I grew up and where I still live, flowers and quilts were the two main means women had of satisfying their hunger for color, so a flower design for a quilt seemed most suitable.

Eunice McAlexander

My mother-in-law made this Double Wedding Ring quilt for my husband's "God Knows When" chest. After we were married we used it on our bed for thirty-five years and just about wore it out.

Billie Dowling Aymett

◆ ◆ ◆ ◆ ◆ ◆ ◆

Great-great-grandmother Polly Ann Kinkead loaned her Feathered Star quilt to a Confederate soldier when he hid in a cave behind the house to escape capture. It wasn't found until some years later, reminding the maker of her part in history.

Maryana S. Huff

◆ ◆ ◆ ◆ ◆ ◆ ◆

Quilting is a way of expressing myself, of sorting out thoughts and emotions, of sifting through daily experiences, frustrations, and joys, to produce a visual, tactile record of a day, a month, a minute. . . . It is a way to wrap my children in love at night, to delight them during the day. Quilting . . . has given me self-confidence and helped me to see that I am a unique individual with a unique view of life.

Katharine R. Brainard

◆ ◆ ◆ ◆ ◆ ◆ ◆

There should be more fun and laughs in quilting. I enjoy it when my quilts raise a smile.

Dorothy Stapleton

◆ ◆ ◆ ◆ ◆ ◆ ◆

Creating quilts is an expression of myself. It is so rewarding to have a lovely heirloom made by my own hands.

Ruby Hinshaw

◆ ◆ ◆ ◆ ◆ ◆ ◆

My grandmother lived with us when I was in high school. She had pieced quilts all of her life, and one day announced that she and I were going to make a quilt. I had taken sewing in home economics, but wasn't overly enthusiastic about learning to quilt. My mother encouraged me to do it because Grandma needed to be needed; she was used to being busy. I filled the gap and got hooked on quilting.

Elsie Vredenburg

There's a mystique surrounding quiltmaking. The excitement of designing our own work; the challenge of tackling a complicated pattern; the sense of accomplishment with each new finished project; the fellowship with other quilters; the fulfillment of sharing our techniques with others; the joy of seeing our work exhibited; and a link to the women of the past are just a few pleasures of quilting.

Judy Sogn

◆ ◆ ◆ ◆ ◆ ◆

I grew up on a farm as one of ten children and my father raised cotton. We planted, hoed, and picked our cotton, and loaded it on the two-horse wagon to go to the gin. My father paid for fertilizer and bought our school shoes and clothes for the winter with the cotton money. Then Mama would take the children and pick the last of the "yellow-scrap-cotton, shirt-tails" to go into the quilts.

Mrs. T. W. Redding, Sr.

◆ ◆ ◆ ◆ ◆ ◆

It is said that women in the United States began quiltmaking not just to save valuable cloth, but also to express affection and consideration for their families. Knowing that, I became involved with quiltmaking as a way to express myself.

Emiko Nagai

When I was a child, I talked to my grandmother about the brooch she wore. I can still recall things she said about it. She told me the pin was the cross of love. . . . I am a grandmother now. I hope I can be as good and loving to my grandson as my grandmother was to me. I inherited so much love from her, and by doing this quilt design [Grandmother's Brooch of Love], I hope to pass some of that love on to my grandson.

Edith Hunter

◆ ◆ ◆ ◆ ◆ ◆ ◆

My learning to quilt has much to do with my grandmother. When she was very ill, I traveled south to spend three weeks with her. She soon regained some of her strength, and before long began to ask for her box of "quilting." She would finger the tiny pieces, and then fall asleep, holding the box.

Diane S. Hire

◆ ◆ ◆ ◆ ◆ ◆ ◆

I can remember watching Mother and Grandmother piece this quilt. They used scraps left from their dresses and the pieces all mean something to me.

Elizabeth Cunningham

My grandmother made her quilts in her bedroom which was so small that the quilting frame formed a low canopy over her bed. . . . When she was ill she would sit in bed like Matisse and sew on the designs. Since she stayed in her room making these quilts . . . there must have been moments of fantasy, memories, and other thoughts to fill the mental space.

David Schirm

◆ ◆ ◆ ◆ ◆ ◆ ◆

My whole life is in that quilt. It scares me some-times when I look at it. All my joys and all my sorrows are stitched into those little pieces. When I was proud of the boys and when I was downright provoked and angry with them. When the girls annoyed me or when they gave me a warm feeling around my heart. And John too. He was stitched into that quilt and all the thirty years we were married. Sometimes I loved him and sometimes I sat there hating him as I pieced the patches together. So they are all in that quilt, my hopes and fears, my joys and sor-rows, my loves and hates. I tremble sometimes when I remember what that quilt knows about me.

Great-grandmother of Marguerite Ickis

So we quilted and rolled, talked and laughed, got
one quilt done, and put in another. The work was not
fine; we laid it out by chalking around a small plate.
Aunt Sally's desire was rather to get her quilting finished
upon this great occasion than for us to put in a quantity
of fine needlework. About five o'clock we were called to
supper. I need not tell you all the particulars of this plen-
tiful meal; but the stewed chicken was tender and we had
coffee again.

Mrs. P. G. Gibbons

◆　◆　◆　◆　◆　◆　◆

The good wives of New England, impressed with
that thrifty orthodoxy of economy which forbids to waste
the merest trifle, had a habit of saving every scrap clipped
out in the fashioning of household garments, and these
they cut into fanciful patterns and constructed of them
rainbow shapes and quaint traceries, the arrangement of
which became one of their few fine arts. . . .

Collections of these tiny fragments were always
ready to fill an hour when there was nothing else to do;
and as the maiden chattered with her beau, her busy flying
needle stitched together those pretty bits, which, little in
themselves, were destined, by gradual unions and accre-
tions, to bring about at last substantial beauty, warmth,
and comfort.

Harriet Beecher Stowe

These people had no carpets for their floor nor curtains for their windows, but they had a rare collection of home-made quilts, some of which were old and worn, but all I thought very beautiful. . . . I could not walk over this carpet of quilts to my bed without first removing my shoes and by the candlelight that night I studied the designs and color combinations in perhaps ten or twelve of them. I doubt if I shall ever have the privilege of sleeping in such surroundings again, and if the sight of a patchwork quilt does not stir in me anything more than the recollection of the experience in this lovely scene it does quite enough.

Allen H. Eaton

◆ ◆ ◆ ◆ ◆ ◆ ◆

There are times a quilt's a way of sayin' "welcome"— a quilt for a new neighbor, or a new bride, or a new baby. We been doin' that sort of thing all our lives.

Lincoln County quilter

I've always had the name o' bein' a good housekeeper, but when I'm dead and gone there ain't anybody goin' to think o' the floors I've swept, and the tables I've scrubbed, and the old clothes I've patched, and the stockin's I've darned. . . . But when one o' my grandchildren or great-grandchildren sees one o' these quilts, they'll think about Aunt Jane, and, wherever I am then, I'll know I ain't forgotten.

Eliza Calvert Hall

When I was growing up my mother was part of a quilting circle. The first time I ever quilted was a project for school on Colonial times. My mother helped me piece a quilt block. When my nephew Joseph was born I made a crib quilt for him. My sister-in-law tells me he's become very attached to it, sometimes using it to make a tent for make believe play. It gives me a good feeling to know that he's so fond of the quilt and that it's taken on a life of its own since it left my hands.

Kathy Nadel

Oh, don't you remember the babes in the wood,
Who were lost and bewildered and crying for food,
And the robins who found them, thinking them dead,
Covered them over with leaves brilliant red
And russet and orange and silver and gilt?
Well! that was the very first crazy-patch quilt.
Flo E. Flintjer

Life is like a patchwork quilt
And each little patch is a day,
Some patches are rosy, happy and bright,
And some are dark and gray.

But each little patch as it's fitted in
And sewn to keep it together
Makes a finished block in this life of ours
Filled with sun, and with rainy weather.

So let me work on Life's patchwork quilt
Through the rainy days and the sun—
Trusting that when I have finished my block
The Master may say: "Well done."
Elizabeth Ryan DeCoursey

What with rearin' a family, and tendin' to a home, and all my chores—that quilt was a long time in the frame. The story of my life is pieced into it. All my joys and all my sorrows.

Lincoln County quilter

The quilt, that most anonymous of women's arts, rarely dated or signed, summarizes more than any other form the major themes in a woman's life—its beginnings, endings, and celebrations retold in bits of colored cloth. In bridal quilts, patchwork coverlets for daily use, parlor quilts, album quilts . . . even in widows' quilts—a woman said everything she knew about art and life.

From *Anonymous Was a Woman*

QUILTERS' WISDOM

Quilting is something I would do even if it was forbidden by law. It's always there in the back of my mind. I work through a lot of things in my mind when I am doing handwork on my quilts. Quilt making gives me the freedom to be creative.

Ivy Tuttle

❖ ❖ ❖ ❖ ❖ ❖ ❖

Our grandmother sat both of us down at the head of the quilt and warned us: "Learn to take pretty little stitches . . . because you're going to have to wake up and look at them every morning!"

Karoline Patterson Bresenhan and
Nancy O'Bryant Puentes

❖ ❖ ❖ ❖ ❖ ❖ ❖

The gift for quilting is like the gift for music. You have to love it. It's *borned* in you. You have to want to create beautiful things. If you've got it—well, you just naturally make things that are beautiful.

Mrs. Blanche Griffith

Quilts are timeless, so people identify with them. When people look at my quilt art, the only thing I hope for is to hear a quick intake of breath because it has been taken away!

Flo Burghardt

◆ ◆ ◆ ◆ ◆ ◆ ◆

If my quilt could talk, it would shout from its distant mountaintops, "Life is beautiful! Rejoice in each new day!" This is the credo of a cancer survivor. This is my credo.

Pat Matthews

◆ ◆ ◆ ◆ ◆ ◆ ◆

Quilting has been a vehicle I've used to meet people throughout the country . . . I could not quilt if I could not share.

Bettina Havig

◆ ◆ ◆ ◆ ◆ ◆ ◆

Quilting feeds me; I can't express myself unless I quilt. It's like I let a secret part of myself out for others to see.

Patti Cunningham

◆ ◆ ◆ ◆ ◆ ◆ ◆

I worry about my quilts, about everyone's quilts. If you collect quilts, you are their guardian. Certain quilts *must* be protected.

Sandy Mitchell

◆ ◆ ◆ ◆ ◆ ◆ ◆

I make quilts for myself, but I'd like others to see the risk I take with color and fabric and perhaps notice something special in my work. If my quilts arouse any kind of emotion, I have been successful.

Sheila R. Chapman

◆ ◆ ◆ ◆ ◆ ◆ ◆

Quilting is always in my mind and it's usually not very subconscious.

Melody Crust

◆ ◆ ◆ ◆ ◆ ◆ ◆

To quilt is a luxury. It allows a few moments for creativity. When I began this quilt, I wanted to disregard the element of time. How long it would take or how many pieces it needed was not my main concern. I felt the more energy I put into the quilt, the more the quilt would speak for itself.

Maggie Potter

My quilts stay in my imagination all of the time.
Heather W. Tewell

❖ ❖ ❖ ❖ ❖ ❖ ❖

Some quilts may be able to talk, but this quilt can sing!
Judith Thompson

❖ ❖ ❖ ❖ ❖ ❖ ❖

Quiltmaking is full of contrasts. It's so easy to learn, but I find it endlessly complex to master.
Deirdre Amsden

❖ ❖ ❖ ❖ ❖ ❖ ❖

Quilting is for me. Life is much fuller, better, and happier since quilting.
Arthur A. Bluj

❖ ❖ ❖ ❖ ❖ ❖ ❖

Quilting is the one thing that has never let me down. It can calm me down or perk me up. And the more quilting on a quilt, the better I like it.
Karen Sikes Collins

I just love to do quilting. Nothing could be finer than to quilt in my recliner in the evening.
JoAnn Brandt

◆ ◆ ◆ ◆ ◆ ◆ ◆

My Grandma told me once that life was just a patchwork quilt, of births and deaths and marriages and things, and sometimes when you're looking for a lovely piece of red you can find a knot of faded strings.
Natalie Whitted Price

Making a friend is a lot like making a quilt.
Margie Boesch

◆ ◆ ◆ ◆ ◆ ◆ ◆

Quilts tell us about their makers with every thread.
Karoline Patterson Bresenhan and
Nancy O'Bryant Puentes

Dishes washed become dirty; food cooked is consumed; a quilt endures.

American Quilts: A Handmade Legacy

❖ ❖ ❖ ❖ ❖ ❖ ❖

Quilting brings together everything I love: fabric, color, mathematics, design, poetry, music. I find there is no end to my satisfaction with making quilts.

Marilyn Henrion

❖ ❖ ❖ ❖ ❖ ❖ ❖

I was in grade school when I learned to sew.
My mother taught me. I learned to quilt before I learned to piece. I was so much a tomboy, Mom had to use strategy to get me to piece a quilt, so she let me use the light colors.

Sarah, an Amish woman

❖ ❖ ❖ ❖ ❖ ❖ ❖

I keep wanting to make quilts that are like bouquets of roses to give away.

Vikki Chenette

We all liked Quilter's Choice because we saw the designs the other club members were working on and swapped scraps of material. There wasn't a quilt top turned out by a member of the Persian Pickle Club that didn't have fabrics from all of us in it. That made us all a part of one another's quilts, just like we were part of one another's lives.

Sandra Dallas,
The Persian Pickle Club

◆ ◆ ◆ ◆ ◆ ◆ ◆

Quilting gives me the pleasure and sense of peace and joy of creating; it preserves my sanity. I hope to live long enough to use up my collection of fabrics.

Sandy McLeon

YOU KNOW YOU'RE A QUILTER WHEN . . .

...you walk into the local restaurant and your daughter takes a look at the floor and says "Look mommy a quilt pattern!"

◆ ◆ ◆ ◆ ◆ ◆ ◆

...you look at the skirt of the person next to you in an elevator and envision it cut into 6-inch squares.

◆ ◆ ◆ ◆ ◆ ◆ ◆

...there's more fabric in the house than food.

◆ ◆ ◆ ◆ ◆ ◆ ◆

...your family buys you "quilt" gifts (fabrics, scissors, tools and toys) for birthday and Christmas.

◆ ◆ ◆ ◆ ◆ ◆ ◆

...your trash never has fabric scraps larger than 1-inch by 1-inch in it.

...you pet fabric.

◆ ◆ ◆ ◆ ◆ ◆ ◆

..."fat quarter" doesn't mean the
heaviest part of your body.

◆ ◆ ◆ ◆ ◆ ◆ ◆

...your first thought when someone
announces they're expecting is,
"What kind of baby quilt should I make?"

◆ ◆ ◆ ◆ ◆ ◆ ◆

...you love all cats, but have a special place
in your heart for calicos.

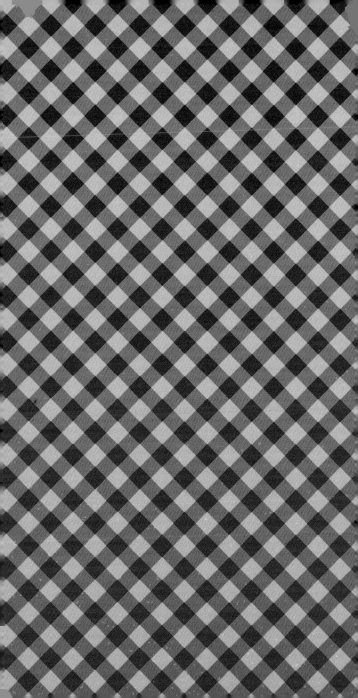